The Charge of the Light Brigade

Famous Cavalry Charge

By Charles River Editors

William Simpson's painting of the Charge of the Light Brigade

About Charles River Editors

Charles River Editors provides superior editing and original writing services across the digital publishing industry, with the expertise to create digital content for publishers across a vast range of subject matter. In addition to providing original digital content for third party publishers, we also republish civilization's greatest literary works, bringing them to new generations of readers via ebooks.

Sign up here to receive updates about free books as we publish them, and visit Our Kindle Author Page to browse today's free promotions and our most recently published Kindle titles.

Introduction

Richard Caton Woodville's painting of the Charge of the Light Brigade

The Charge of the Light Brigade

"'Forward, the Light Brigade!'

Was there a man dismay'd?

Not tho' the soldier knew

Someone had blunder'd:

Theirs not to make reply,

Theirs not to reason why,

Theirs but to do and die:

Into the valley of Death

Rode the six hundred." – Lord Tennyson, "The Charge of the Light Brigade"

The Charge of the Light Brigade is the most famous British cavalry charge in history, possibly also eclipsing the renown of any other mounted attack conducted by the armed forces of other nations in the general imagination. This cavalry action is certainly remembered far more vividly than the 1854 Battle of Balaclava during which it occurred, and even the wider Crimean War that led to the battle.

Of course, the prominence of the Charge in popular and historical memory is due primarily to Alfred, Lord Tennyson's poem describing the events of that distant late October afternoon. The bearded Poet Laureate crafted a powerful, gripping poetic narrative that fixed the encounter firmly in both the popular imagination and in the English literary oeuvre. Millions of people who know nothing else of the Crimean War between Great Britain and the Russian Empire are familiar with Tennyson's memorable verses:

> "Half a league, half a league,
>
> Half a league onward,
>
> All in the valley of Death,
>
> Rode the six hundred.
>
> 'Forward the Light Brigade!
>
> 'Charge for the guns!' he said:
>
> Into the valley of Death
>
> Rode the six hundred."

Tennyson's work is a magnificent achievement of verbal art, filled with the violent energy of battle and providing a glimpse of the living men who carried out the desperate action more than a century and a half ago. Filled with the thunder of artillery and the hurtling momentum of lancers and hussars flinging themselves upon the enemy, Tennyson's poem is simultaneously a triumphant celebration of the Light Brigade's valor and a lament for their futile sacrifice in the teeth of concentrated Russian cannon salvos.

At the same time, however, his words also created a narrative about the combat which has obscured much contrary evidence, replacing fact with legend and completely obscuring the true significance of the Charge of the Light Brigade. Indeed, its perception by historians and depiction in history books has been massively influenced by the sheer artistic power of Tennyson's poem. Sober historians have unwitting cherry-picked the existing original documents to support Tennyson's "version" of the events while disregarding much contrary evidence that provides a very different perspective of the Light Brigade's attack.

In fact, a closer examination of source materials casts the Charge of the Light Brigade in a very different light than the widely accepted version of men so highly disciplined and obedient that they obeyed a suicidal order without question. So unquestioningly obedient were the British cavalrymen, the legend declares, that they were willing to charge into a cannon's mouth and die rather than raise a voice of protest against the imbecility of their incompetent officers. This mix of doomed courage and absolute, unfaltering compliance with the orders of their superiors, however idiotic, had given the Light Brigade and the British soldier in general a character of tragic heroism. This acquiescence to authority is often extended to Lord Cardigan, the unit's commander, as well.

Once the order had been given by the overall commander Lord Raglan, Tennyson's poem would have readers believe Cardigan then chose an incorrect objective and pursued it with dogged obedience to what he thought were his orders. The Light Brigade obeyed him in turn, and the result was an attack whose deterministic momentum could not be halted even when certain individuals realized it was an error and sought to halt or redirect it.

Powerful as this vision of buffoonish commanders leading soldiers infused with ant-like obedience may be in the world of poetry, considerable documentation still exists which at least partially refutes such an interpretation. These documents, recently revisited by a handful of historians, greatly diminish the role of upper-echelon mistakes in causing the Charge. They restore agency and initiative to the ordinary British soldiers, highlighting them as fierce, independent-minded, and energetic actors in their own right, who very nearly changed the outcome of the entire Battle of Balaclava with their skill, courage, and daring.

Ironically, it is possible to argue that the Charge of the Light Brigade was an attack mostly initiated by the rank and file, and that it was largely successful. The actual blunder was the failure of other commanders to support the charge by sending in infantry in its wake, which could potentially have led to the complete rout of the Russian forces. Instead, the British commanders did nothing to exploit the breakthrough created by the initiative, skill, and ferocity of the ordinary cavalryman, squandering the opportunity they had been offered.

Ultimately, these men were to seize on Tennyson's version of events because it portrayed them as responsible for a relatively small blunder (the needless sacrifice of a few hundred men, which still underlined the martial pride of British courage) rather than a colossal one (throwing away a chance to soundly defeat the entire Russian army, thus permitting the battle to end as a bloody, pointless stalemate).

. *The Charge of the Light Brigade* chronicles the history and legacy of the ill-fated cavalry charge. Along with pictures of important people, places, and events, you will learn about the Charge of the Light Brigade like never before, in no time at all.

The Charge of the Light Brigade: The History and Legacy of Europe's Most Famous Cavalry Charge

About Charles River Editors

Introduction

Chapter 1: The Origins of the Crimean War

Understanding the Charge of the Light Brigade requires it to be placed in the context of the larger conflict that served as its stage. In fact, a unique combination of factors led to the British cavalry launching itself furiously against the Russian artillery and the Cossack cavalry lurking beyond on October 25th, 1854, and the conditions of the Crimean War created a set of stresses and difficulties which prompted the British cavalry to respond in a specific manner to developments on the Balaclava battlefield.

The purported cause of the Crimean War lay in fatal skirmishes between Orthodox and Catholic monks in Jerusalem, which Czar Nicholas I blamed on the Ottoman Empire extending insufficient protection to Eastern Orthodox pilgrims. There is no doubt that the Orthodox did suffer greater casualties in this bizarre religious vendetta, but the waning of Ottoman Turkish power and Russian ambitions towards expansion into the Black Sea region and the Eastern Mediterranean were likely the chief motivating force behind the Czar's aggression.

Czar Nicholas I

In a discussion with Sir George H. Seymour, the British ambassador to Russia, Czar Nicholas revealed his obsession with the collapse of the Ottoman Empire. Speaking to the envoy on January 9, 1853, the Czar referred to Turkey as "the bear" and stated that the "bear dies... the bear is dying... you may give him musk but even musk will not long keep him alive." (Temperley, 1936, 272). This phrase was later erroneously interpolated by the newspapers of the era into the famous description of the Ottoman Empire as "the sick man of Europe."

Czar Nicholas I clearly wished for this to be the case, and he further stated that he wanted no resurgent "Byzantine Empire" in the form of a powerful Greek state in Turkey's place. As with Vladimir Putin's invasion of the Crimea and eastern Ukraine a century and a half later, Russia's foreign policy was predicated on the imperative of fomenting weakness, instability, and fragmentation among its neighbors. This strategy was (and still is) designed to remove potential obstacles to Russian imperialism and to provide suitable pretexts for intervention in other nearby countries when desired by the rulers of the Muscovite state.

Ultimately, the Czar launched an attack on the Turks, allegedly due to the killing of Orthodox pilgrims in the Holy Land but actually to further Russian aggrandizement in the Black Sea and Eastern Mediterranean regions. The Russians defeated the Ottomans decisively at the naval battle of Sinope, while sending land forces into Moldova, then a Turkish possession. France, Great Britain, and the Kingdom of Sardinia felt their trading interests threatened by this maneuver, and they also feared Russian expansion in the direction of western Europe. Accordingly, the British and French intervened to save the Ottoman Empire from dismemberment by Russia, leading to the start of the Crimean War in 1854.

This conflict was quite controversial with the British public, but it did succeed in its chief objective of preventing Russian destruction of the Turkish realm at that time. It is one of the bizarre ironies of history that the Ottoman Empire would survive until the end of World War I, when the very British army that had preserved it two and a half generations earlier proved to be the instrument of its final destruction.

Chapter 2: The Siege of Sevastopol

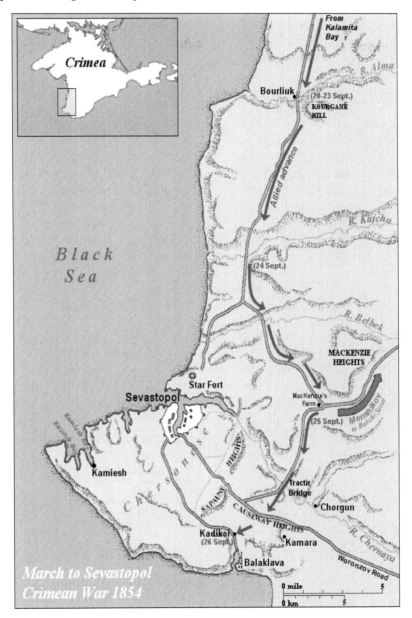

The location of Sevastopol in the Crimea

In a counterstroke to the Czar's aggression, a coalition army of British, French, and Turkish soldiers landed in Crimea and, after defeating the Russian forces at the Battle of the Alma, moved to besiege the port city of Sevastopol. This decision was bitterly mocked by the late British novelist George MacDonald Fraser in his novel *Flashman at the Charge*, in which he wrote, "It struck me then, and still does, that attacking Sevastopol would be rather like an enemy of England investing Penzance, and then shouting towards London, 'There, you insolent bastard, that'll teach you!' But because it was said to be a great base, and The Times was full of it, an assault on Sevastopol became the talk of the hour." (Fraser, 1986, 28).

In this passage, Fraser echoed the current common belief that the Crimean War was an exercise in absurdity at all levels, including strategic planning. However, while ample incompetence was displayed throughout the conflict, the siege of Sevastopol was one case where the criticism appears unfair. The Crimean War has become a sort of theatrical and allegorical performance rather than history in the popular mind, and while aspects of the Charge of the Light Brigade have metamorphosed into patriotic myths, the cartoonish incompetence of the British government and army has also become mythologized, creating a huge mass of emotionally-charged exaggerations on a slender foundation of historical reality. The reality is that the alliance of Britain, France, Sardinia, and the Turks did not seek the wholesale defeat of Russia. Rather, it was attempting to force the Russians to abandon two threatening objectives: the destruction of the Ottoman Empire and the establishment of a powerful Russian naval presence in the Black Sea and eastern Mediterranean.

Since Sevastopol was the main Russian port in the region, striking at it was actually a shrewd, robust strategic decision on the part of the Allied command. The acuity of the Allies' strategic thinking is again underlined by the renewed Russian aggression in the region in 2014. Vladimir Putin's imperial ambitions led him to seize the Crimea and the port of Sevastopol in particular, by using direct annexation and open military force rather than the disguised Russian soldiers used elsewhere in Ukraine to create plausible deniability. Precisely 160 years later, Sevastopol is still considered the key strategic position for regional naval dominance by the Russian military and civil leadership.

Franz Roubaud's painting depicting the siege

Though attacking Sevastopol was a sound strategic decision in terms of the Crimean War's objectives, the actual execution left much to be desired, even as the siege interested foreign observers like American engineer George McClellan, who witnessed the siege and was heavily influenced by it when pressing his own campaigns during the American Civil War. The forces sent were too small to launch an all-out attack on Sevastopol and seize it outright, which led to investing the fortress instead for a protracted siege. This circumstance had fatal consequences for the Allied army because forcing the men to remain in one place led to massive outbreaks of disease. Germs eventually wiped out a major percentage of the expeditionary force amid almost inconceivable scenes of human misery and suffering.

In addition to damage inflicted by appalling pre-modern hygiene conditions and poorly organized supply deliveries, the Russians made multiple attempts to break the encirclement of Sevastopol. One of these efforts led to the Battle of Balaclava, during which the Charge of the Light Brigade was the day's last and most spectacular action. Balaclava was the site of the harbor the British used to resupply their besieging force, while the French used the much more practical Kamiesch. According to Frances "Fanny" Duberly, the wife of a British officer who kept a diary of the campaign, "[A]t morning, the *Simla* came to tow us to our anchorage just outside

Balaklava harbour. This anchorage is a wonderful place; the water is extremely deep, and the rocks which bound the coast exceed in ruggedness and boldness of outline any that I ever saw before. The harbour appears completely land-locked. Through a fissure in the cliffs you can just see a number of masts; but how they got in, or will get out, appears a mystery; they have the appearance of having been hoisted over the cliffs, and dropped into a lake on the other side." (Duberly, 2007, 73-74).

Its picturesque aspects aside, Balaclava harbor was a rather poor choice as a supply point. It was vulnerable to storms from the south, as well as possible attack by Russian vessels. Additionally, the route from the harbor to the siegeworks around Sevastopol was poorly developed. The British commissariat was supposed to supply enormous quantities of preserved food, but ultimately, most of this would end up piling up on the beach and rot due to lack of adequate transport arrangements between the harbor and the siegeworks. Thousands of British soldiers would eventually starve to death despite the fact incredible quantities of food were stockpiled only a few miles distant.

However, these dismal failures still lay in the future when Fanny Duberly arrived. At that point, supplies were flowing through Balaclava to the besieging force at Sevastopol. The Russian commanders judged that the best way to defeat the Allied force entirely was not to engage it head-on but to strike at Balaclava, seizing the harbor and cutting off supplies. Their plan, if successful, would have had the effect of isolating the force investing Sevastopol, thus compelling its retreat or surrender. Naturally, the Allied forces perceived this risk and deployed to protect their supply lines, setting the stage for the Battle of Balaclava on October 25th, 1854. British soldiers formed the backbone of this defense, but Turkish and French units were also present on the field. Interestingly, though relatively few in numbers in the field, both the French and the Turks would have an important effect on the development of the Light Brigade's role in the day's events.

An 1855 picture of the port of Balaclava

Chapter 3: Prelude to Battle

The Russian commander, General Pavel Liprandi (a Russian of Italian descent) later proved himself a smooth liar and spinner of reassuring fantasies in reporting to the Imperial court about the battle, but he had a fairly realistic grasp of the relative positions of the two armies. He perceived that Balaclava was both a tactically crucial point whose seizure might enable him to establish a chokehold on British supply lines and also a relatively weak point with only around 4,000 men defending it. Both of these reasons led him to choose Balaclava as the spot for his first thrust in the effort to relieve Sevastopol.

Liprandi

Initially, he did not have enough troops on hand to feel confident of success in attacking the British position, and the earlier Battle of the Alma had proven that British infantry firepower was devastating against the poorly trained and poorly armed Russian forces, even when the latter enjoyed vast numerical superiority and were fighting from prepared positions. The Russians had been soundly crushed fighting a defensive action against inferior numbers, so Liprandi evidently felt he needed many more men if he were to have a chance of success during the even riskier process of mounting an offensive battle.

As a result, the timing of the Battle of Balaclava was determined by the speed with which General Liprandi received his reinforcements. The heavy cavalry of Prince Menshikov continued to probe the British lines throughout October, gathering intelligence and keeping the enemy occupied. The reinforcements Liprandi had requested arrived in the third week of October, and the Russian general felt ready to make his attack on the morning of October 25th, 1854.

Menshikov

Liprandi was under pressure since the bombardment of Sevastopol was proceeding and the British might launch an assault at any time, and a significant event on October 17th might have helped to speed up the Russian general's decision to attack even more. On that date, the Allies opened a cannonade on Sevastopol with 120 guns, a massive outpouring of shells which had a startling effect within a few hours of its commencement and was destined to show how the dilatory and hesitant British command wasted opportunity after opportunity during the Crimean War. Part of the British bombardment fell on the Malikoff Redoubt, a portion of the Sevastopol defenses that housed a gigantic ammunition dump and powder magazine. Fanny Duberly recounted what happened next in her journal, referring to the Malikoff Redoubt as the "Redan" (a French term for a salient earthwork facing the enemy): "At ten minutes past three a magnificent sight presented itself – a huge explosion in the Mud Fort (Redan), the smoke of which ascended to the eye of heaven, and then gathering, fell slowly and mournfully down to earth…round me, cheers burst from every throat – All down the line one deafening shout." (Kelly, 2007, 86).

From a military standpoint, the destruction of the Malikoff Redoubt should have been a massive victory for the British and a fatal catastrophe to the Russians defending Sevastopol. The guns in this important area of the defenses were ruined or dismounted by the blast, and many men (including the Russian admiral commanding them) were killed. A significant gap had been opened in the defensive works protecting Sevastopol, and the British infantry could have advanced into this breach with impunity, subject to no artillery fire and very little musketry from the stunned defenders. Instead, the Allied command did nothing. Their superb infantry, which had not yet been decimated by disease and starvation, stood idle, with no orders to advance. Had an attack been launched, it is almost certain that Sevastopol would have been taken then and there, on the first day of the main part of the siege. Instead, the British and French would require almost an entire year until September 5th, 1855, the date of a successful attack on the Malikoff Redoubt. Undoubtedly unable to believe his good fortune, the Russians' chief engineer in Sevastopol, a Latvian lieutenant colonel by the name of Eduard Totleben, oversaw a hasty rebuilding of the Redoubt. The salient was rebuilt and rearmed sufficiently to be able to repulse an attack by the following morning, thanks to Totleben's energy and initiative. With that, the opportunity had slipped through the Allies' fingers.

Over the ensuing few days, other portions of Sevastopol's defensive works were blown up, yet no attack was ever made on the gaps subsequently produced. Fanny Duberly noted that there was considerable "talk" of storming the town, but she guessed shrewdly that the amount of discussion indicated there would be no action. She also correctly anticipated that the army would remain encamped around Sevastopol throughout the winter instead of exploit any breakthroughs made.

Sir George Cathcart, the British infantry commander, later claimed that the attacks were not made because of difficulties in coordinating with his French allies. Though this excuse had a superficial gloss of plausibility, the name of Cathcart emerged again during the Charge of the Light Brigade, demonstrating the same pattern of being unable to follow up on even the most evident opportunities.

Cathcart

Chapter 4: The Thin Red Line and the Heavy Brigade

On the morning of October 25th, 1854, General Liprandi advanced his forces of cavalry, infantry, and artillery against the Allied soldiers defending Balaclava. The bulk of these defensive forces were British, but a number of Turks and a few French units were also present. Two brigades of British cavalry – the Heavy Brigade and the Light Brigade – were on the field, as were the 92nd Highland Infantry and various other infantry units. Together, the British, Ottomans, and French fielded 4,500 men and 26 guns, while General Liprandi was advancing with 25,000 men and 78 guns. Overall, Allied command lay with General Sir Fitzroy Somerset, 1st Baron Raglan (usually known simply as Raglan). The Cavalry Division, which included both the Light and Heavy Brigades, was commanded by Lieutenant General George Bingham, 3rd Earl of Lucan (generally called Lucan).

Raglan

Lucan

The weather on October 25th, 1854 was superbly clear, providing excellent visibility, and the dry ground was well suited to cavalry maneuvers. The battlefield, despite certain complexities, basically consisted of two valleys with heights on the south, in the center (separating the two valleys), and on the north. The Fedioukine Heights formed the northern edge of the battlefield, fringing the North Valley on that side. The Causeway Heights were a towering ridge which ran west to east, dividing the North Valley from the South Valley. In the south were hills around Balaclava itself, providing the southern limit of the South Valley. The Sapoune Heights stood at the western end of both valleys.

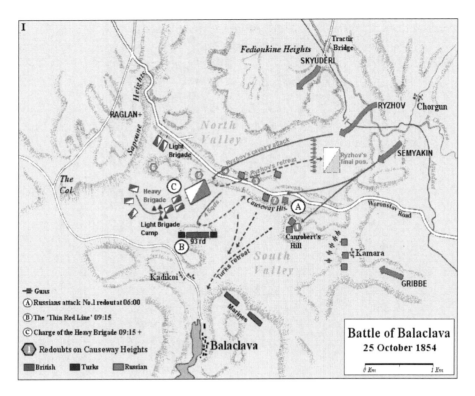

Map of the Battle of Balaclava

At the beginning of the battle, the Ottoman forces held a series of five redoubts along the crest of the Causeway Heights. A sixth redoubt stood on Canrobert's Hill, an eminence at the east end of the Causeway Heights. These redoubts, or small forts, were fitted with cannons taken from the British ship HMS *Diamond* and were intended to have a commanding position overlooking the North Valley as the first line of defense for Balaclava harbor in the south.

British cavalry was present at the extreme western end of both the North and South Valleys, just under the commanding Sapoune Heights. The Light Brigade was deployed at the western end of the North Valley, and the Heavy Brigade was at the western end of the South Valley. The 93rd Highlanders were deployed on a hill just north of Balaclava on the south side of the South Valley, with several units of Royal Marines supporting their right (eastern) flank on the hills there. The Sapoune Heights themselves were held by French and British infantry forces.

The Russian forces approached from the northeast across the Fedioukine Heights, with some elements advancing directly from the east. These forces moved forward through the predawn darkness over extremely difficult terrain, which could possibly have led to them starting the battle already fatigued. At around first light, the Russians forces flowed down from the

Fedioukine Heights in the north into the eastern end of the North Valley, and from there, they attacked up the slopes of the Causeway Heights towards the Turkish positions around Redoubts numbers 1, 2, and 3. This line of attack kept them well clear of the British cavalry assets at the western end of the valley, which might otherwise have launched a flank attack on them.

The Russian attack was carried out in three prongs, which moved with surprising coordination considering the mediocre quality of Czarist officers and poorly trained conscripts. Several additional forces moved up as support or waited in reserve, some of which were destined to engage the Light Brigade during its famous charge.

The leftmost prong, which advanced straight from the east, was commanded by Major General Gribbe and consisted of 3,000 men and 10 cannons. This detachment advanced to seize the village of Kamara at the extreme eastern end of the Causeway Heights and assisted in attacking Redoubt 1 on Canrobert's Hill. Meanwhile, Major Generals Semiakin and Levutski commanded a heavy central column consisting of 8,000 men and 18 cannons, including the Ukraine Regiment, the Azov Regiment, the Dnieper Regiment, and elements of the No. 4 Rifle Battalion. The right-hand prong was led by Colonel Skiuderi and included the Odessa Regiment, the No. 53 Don Cossacks, and a company from the No. 4 Rifle Battalion, totaling 4,000 men and 12 cannons. These attacks were supported by a detached cavalry force of 3,000 sabers and 16 cannons commanded by Lieutenant General Rhyzhov, and included the Kiev Cavalry Regiment, the Ingermanland Cavalry Regiment, and the No. 1 Ural Cossacks. Additional reserve units incorporated at least 7,000 infantry and cavalry and a further 22 cannons.

The Turks in the redoubts soon spotted the gray-coated hordes pouring down from the northern and eastern hills, and they raised signal flags on the redoubts to alert the British. Lucan sent a warning to Raglan, who had dismissed evidence of an attack as enemy disinformation the evening before, but now he deployed the Heavy Brigade in a threatening demonstration. Though they were kept well clear of the Russian infantry columns, they could repulse cavalry if they kept good order.

Lucan had hoped to stop or at least delay the Russians through threat of a flank cavalry attack, but the Czarist commanders ignored his cavalry entirely. The dense columns of Russian infantry trudged stolidly forward in their heavy gray coats under a sparkling forest of bayonets. In the meantime, the Russian artillery deployed and began to pour a heavy supporting fire against the redoubts along the crest of the ridge.

The Ottomans, already displaying slovenly military discipline, had neglected to clear the bushes and trees from around their redoubts, and thus they had poor fields of fire against the advancing Russians. Gribbe's men attacked Redoubt 1 first, exterminating most of its cowering defenders without resistance and sending the rest fleeing to the other redoubts. Not surprisingly, the panic of the survivors from Redoubt 1 spread like a plague among the other Turkish soldiers across the length of the Causeway Heights. In fact, the Ottoman soldiers did not wait for the arrival of the Russians but simply plundered their own positions for any portable loot and then fled west and south, seeking the safety of the British lines or Balaclava harbor itself. Fanny Duberly, who was riding hard to get a view of the battle, encountered the fleeing Turks and noted with a mixture of pity and contempt, "The road was almost blocked up with flying Turks, some running hard … while others came along laden with pots, kettles, arms, and plunder of every description, chiefly old bottles, for which the Turks appear to have a great appreciation." (Kelly, 2007, 92).

It was at this juncture that a small but significant incident occurred, one which contributed to the developments leading to the Charge of the Light Brigade. Some of the Turks were not so lucky as to escape along the road with blankets, cooking pots, and the much-prized glass bottles, and Sergeant-Major George Loy Smith of the Light Brigade left this account of what happened next: "As [the Turks] gained the plain, a number of Cossacks swept around the foot of the hill, killing and wounding many of them. Some of them, unarmed, raised their hands imploringly, but it was only to have them severed from their bodies. This we had to witness close in front of our squadrons, feeling the while that had a dozen or two of us been sent out numbers of these poor fellows might have been saved." (Loy Smith, 1987, 126).

British culture at the time stressed fair play and included a strong anathema towards those who killed men trying to surrender. Thus, the sight of the Cossacks butchering the Turks while these defeated soldiers begged for their lives enraged the men of the Light Brigade. Loy Smith reports that their fury rose even higher when the Cossacks, having finished massacring the luckless Turks under the very noses of the Light Brigade, swept around the flank of the British unit and entered their night encampment. There, the Cossack riders found sick horses picketed and unable to escape. These trapped animals were disemboweled or otherwise injured with the Cossacks' lances before they rode away, jeering at the immobile British cavalry and leaving them seething with rage, disgust, and humiliation.

Unaware of the storm brewing on his extreme right flank, Liprandi secured the Causeway Heights, and the Russians were in full possession of the high ridge of land between the North and South Valleys, including all six redoubts, by 8:30 a.m. All of the artillery in the redoubts was also captured, except for three pieces in Redoubt 1 which had been spiked by a British officer serving as an adviser to the Turks.

Thus far, Liprandi's plan had been an almost unqualified success, but this run of good luck for the Russians was about to change drastically. At the time, however, it must have appeared to the Russian command that an easy victory was in their grasp; from the commanding eminence of the Causeway Heights, the harbor of Balaclava was visible to the south in the clear early sunlight. Between the Russians and their objective stood 550 men of the 93rd Highlanders, with some 1,000 Royal Marines deployed on their right flank, but the force of slightly under 1,600 infantry must have appeared puny compared to the tens of thousands of Russian soldiers swarming forward to take the Causeway Heights.

The British, meanwhile, were not entirely passive, but Raglan was slow to react, as he was unable to see exactly how many Russians were advancing and fancied that the attack might be a small raid meant to distract him from a larger assault elsewhere. Considering that Balaclava harbor was the only worthwhile tactical or strategic objective in the area, this seems like a rather foolish conclusion, but it was the one that Raglan acted on. The British commander sent orders to the Duke of Cambridge, commanding the 1st Infantry Division, and Sir George Cathcart, commanding the 4th Infantry Division, to advance into the North and South Valleys in support of the cavalry and the Highlanders. The Duke of Cambridge obeyed the order, but the 1st Infantry Division was encamped miles away near Sevastopol and had a considerable distance to march.

Sir George Cathcart was close by – on the Sapoune Heights, in fact – but he chose to ignore a series of orders prompting him to advance. His behavior was eerily reminiscent of his complete inertia when offered the chance to take Sevastopol after the destruction of the Malikoff Redoubt on October 17th. He later wrote a letter to his wife in which he brazenly lied to her by asserting that his force was six miles away and thus unable to move up quickly, which might indicate that his inaction tormented his conscience, and in fact, he would throw his life away in a suicidal frontal attack two weeks later at the Battle of Inkerman, evidently seeking to exonerate himself from both whispered accusations of cowardice and his own sense of guilt.

In the meantime, Liprandi sent Ryzhov's massive cavalry detachment forward laterally across the Causeway heights, thus entering the South Valley while traveling in a southwesterly direction, but Ryzhov's orders were strangely vague. In an almost Raglan-like display of poor generalship, Liprandi told Ryzhov to take the "enemy's camp," a totally pointless objective since it was currently vacant and was in any case only a small encampment for the Light Brigade. Regardless, Ryzhov moved forward in command of 3,000 cavalry, consisting of the Kiev Regiment of Hussars, the Ingermanland Regiment, and the No 1. Ural Cossacks, and rode down off the Causeway Heights into the South Valley.

The 93rd Highlanders under Sir Colin Campbell had taken refuge on a reverse slope to avoid Russian long-range artillery fire from the Causeway Heights and were no longer visible. Thus, to Ryzhov, it appeared that the way to Kadikoi, a key village near Balaclava Harbor, was completely open, and accordingly, he detached 4 squadrons of Kiev Hussars and a few Cossacks and sent them to take the village. Ryzhov himself led the rest of his mounted thousands southwest, towards the Light Brigade's empty camp.

The action known as the "Thin Red Line" began when the 93rd Highlanders moved back to the crest of the rise they had been hiding behind, appearing as if from nowhere in the path of the four detached Kiev Hussar squadrons. This threw the Russians into confusion, and there is some doubt as to what occurred next. Many historians state that the Highlanders fired at extreme range, wounding some men but failing to cause significant damage to the hussar squadrons. The hussars then retired, having no wish to charge steady infantry.

Robert Gibb's "The Third Red Line"

Contemporary accounts, however, suggest that the action was far more bloody than this. Fanny Duberly describes a scene in which the Kiev Hussars charged the 93rd violently, which seems a likely reaction since Sir Colin Campbell had deployed his men in line rather than the effective anti-cavalry square formation. Infantry in line in the Napoleonic era was highly vulnerable to cavalry, as horses will charge into a line of men, but they often refused to push into a solid square of men presenting a hedge of bayonets at all points.

As a result, it is very likely that the Russian cavalry commanders would have deemed the Highlanders to be poorly deployed, not yet realizing the terrible firepower the British infantry now possessed in the form of the Pattern 1853 Enfield rifle-musket. A line of infantry with smoothbore muskets would be unable to stop a determined cavalry attack, but the precise accuracy and tremendous power of the rifle-musket made an attack on prepared infantry suicidal, even if they were not deployed in a square.

Fanny Duberly provided a vivid vignette of the lethal moment: "Not a man stirred, they stood like rocks till the Russian horses came within about thirty yards – Then one terrific volley – a sudden wheel – a piece of ground strewed with men and horses – when the [Scots Greys and Royal Inniskillings heavy cavalry] bounding from the ranks dashed with their heavy horses on the mounted foe & hewed them down. Ten minutes more and not a live Russian was seen that side the hill." (Kelly, 2007, 93).

Mrs. Duberly's account indicates that the Highlanders held their fire until the Russian hussars were just 100 feet away, then fired a single lethal volley. Two elements of the Heavy Brigade, the 2nd Regiment of Dragoons (or "Scots Greys") and the 6th Regiment of Dragoons (or "Inniskillings") then attacked the flank of the retreating Kiev Hussars and routed them, inflicting heavy casualties.

A letter from the 93rd's Color Sergeant J. Joiner describes a similar scene, but it does not entirely corroborate Mrs. Duberly's account: "Wheeling round they fondly thought of turning our right flank, but we brought our left shoulder round, presenting a new front, caught *them* on the flank, when volley after volley was fired into them so fast, that they could not advance, as their own dead and dying choked their way." (Dawson, 2014, Chapter 4).

Whatever the exact number of volleys, it is clear that multiple eyewitnesses to the action saw the ground choked with dying Russians and horses, making it likely that the hussars were repulsed violently rather than simply turning back while at extreme range. Furthermore, material evidence suggests that the Kiev Hussars were well within lethal range of the Highlanders. A quick glance at any map of the situation reveals that the Causeway Heights were only about 500 yards from the 93rd Highlanders' position, and the Pattern 1853 Enfield rifle-musket was accurate and lethal to 600 yards in the hands of a regular soldier. In fact, it could kill at 900 yards when used by a marksman.

Thus, the Kiev Hussars were within lethal range of the Highlanders as soon as they crested the Causeway Heights, and they were undoubtedly far closer when the Scottish soldiers emerged from cover. At just 200-250 yards, the fire of 550 men armed with the Pattern 1853 Enfield rifle-musket would have been devastating. Therefore, it seems highly improbable that the Hussars escaped without casualties when the very nature of the topography means they were deep inside the lethal range of the Highlanders' weapons when the engagement began.

In the meantime, Ryzhov led the main body of cavalry towards the useless objective of the Light Brigade's camp. The Russian commander soon encountered the entire Heavy Brigade under Brigadier General James Scarlett, and, inexplicably, halted his masses of cavalry. He enjoyed an upslope position, and a brisk charge would likely have rolled up the smaller British force neatly, but instead, Ryzhov sat motionless while Scarlett calmly deployed his cavalry and attacked with them.

William Simpson's painting of the Charge of the Heavy Brigade

Despite having time to form, the Heavy Brigade arrived piecemeal and from multiple directions. The first few units into action were nearly swamped under the weight of Russian numbers, but the Russians were eventually broken as other units of the much smaller Heavy Brigade attacked them furiously from multiple directions. British artillery concentrated accurate fire on the luckless Russian horsemen at about this time, completing the rout.

However, an opportunity to secure a major victory was lost at this point yet again thanks to the inaction of a British commander. Though men of the Light Brigade called for an attack on the retreating Russian cavalry, Cardigan refused to allow them to move, even as he showed every sign of impatience and eagerness himself. Repeating a predictable pattern, yet another English commander failed to seize a golden opportunity to launch a devastating attack that likely would have turned a qualified success into an overwhelming victory.

Cardigan

Chapter 5: The Charge of the Light Brigade Begins

Throughout the morning, the Light Brigade had sat idle, watching the actions of other British units in the distance but failing to participate in the events. On the day of the battle, the Light Brigade, like the Heavy Brigade, was a composite, temporary assemblage of separate units. Five regiments were gathered under the command of James Brudenell, 7th Earl of Cardigan (generally known simply as Cardigan): the 4th Light Dragoons under Lieutenant Colonel Lord George Paget; the 13th Light Dragoons, commanded by Captain John Oldham; the 8th Hussars, led by Lieutenant Colonel Frederick Shewell; the 11th Hussars under Lieutenant Colonel John Douglas; and the 17th Lancers, commanded by Captain William Morris (McGuigan, 2001, 18). The total strength of the Light Brigade stood at 675 officers and men as of the morning muster on October 25th, 1854.

Each type of cavalryman – hussar, light dragoon, and lancer – had their own distinctive uniforms and some variation in equipment. The hussars wore a cylindrical fur busby and a highly decorated coat or pelisse which was worn over the shoulder much of the time rather than actually being donned. These soldiers were equipped with a percussion-lock carbine and a cavalry sword. The light dragoons also carried a percussion-lock carbine and cavalry sword, but they wore a cylindrical cloth hat instead of the fur busby.

The Lancers wore strange-looking Polish-style light helmets and carried a lance and a cavalry sword. Since a carbine interfered with correct lance handling, each man was instead equipped with a single-shot percussion-lock pistol (Chappell, 2002, 15). The lancers were the most prestigious, but ironically, they were also the most impractically armed of the three types of cavalry comprising the Light Brigade at Balaclava.

The mood of the Light Brigade in the mid-to-late morning was very different from the calm, stoic fatalism that Tennyson evoked with his poem. Instead, written accounts suggest that the ordinary horsemen and their officers were enraged, frustrated, and in a fiercely aggressive mood. They were angered by the butchery of the Turks and their sick horses by the Cossacks in the immediate vicinity of their formation, fuming at the fact they were not allowed to join the cavalry action in the South Valley alongside the Heavy Brigade, and in a rebellious state due to lack of action and the jibes of other units at their complete uselessness thus far.

At the same time, Raglan was also growing impatient because the infantry he had ordered forward still had not appeared on the field by the end of the Heavy Brigade's charge at around 9:30 a.m. At approximately 10:15, some 15 minutes before the leading elements of the 1st and 4th infantry divisions descended from the heights, he sent an order to Lucan, overall commander of the British cavalry, which read, "Cavalry to advance and take advantage of any opportunity to recover the Heights. They will be supported by the infantry which has been ordered to advance on two fronts."

Raglan's plan, as it later emerged, was for the 1st Division under the Duke of Cambridge to advance east along the North Valley and assault the Causeway Heights from that direction. The 4th Division under Sir George Cathcart was to advance in tandem along the South Valley. The two divisions would then launch simultaneous attacks up the north and south slopes of the Causeway Heights, driving out the Russians and recapturing the redoubts abandoned by the Turks.

Lucan prepared his squadrons but did not advance as ordered, and for once, this was an act of prudence on his part, as he was not ready to risk his horsemen without the infantry already in place and ready to advance. Since ultimately neither infantry division engaged in serious combat that day, and it eventually fell to a French infantry unit to clear the northerly Fedioukine Heights in the afternoon and precipitate the Russian retreat, his concerns about the usefulness of the British infantry proved justified.

Although it has long been assumed that the Light Brigade had mostly sat idle on the battlefield that morning, some evidence suggests that a number of men from the Light Brigade had already seen action that morning because they deserted their assigned ranks to join the Heavy Brigade. This was vehemently denied by Cardigan and all other ranking officers, but it might have merely been an act of human decency on their part because a soldier leaving his post in a combat situation would be liable to anything from summary disciplinary action to a court-martial and execution. These official denials, meant to shield the ordinary soldiers, have also concealed the reality that it was rowdy, unruly, and adventurous men who made up the Light Brigade, not the obedient, resigned stoics prevalent in Tennyson's poem.

This assertion was bolstered by some accounts written among members of the Heavy Brigade. For example, the assistant surgeon of the Heavy Brigade, William Cattell, reported in a letter: "Several other troopers fell in with our ranks, amongst them two privates of the 11th Hussars who must have been doing a bit on their own hook." (Small, 2007, Chapter 5). It seems apparent that some troopers from the Light Brigade deserted their units temporarily in order to get into the thick of the action in the earlier half of the morning.

There is an even more startling assertion by Private John Doyle, who claimed that much of the Light Brigade actually charged without orders when Ryzhov's cavalry was repulsed by the Heavy Brigade: "The Light Brigade were not well pleased when they saw the Heavy Brigade charge and were not let go to their assistance. They stood up in their stirrups, and shouted 'Why are we kept here?' and at the same moment [...] dashed back through our lines, for the purpose of following the Russian retreat, but they had got too far for us to overtake them." (Small, 2007, Chapter 5). If this account is true, and there seems little reason for Doyle to lie, the famous Charge of the Light Brigade may actually have been the second charge made by the unit that day. The first was an abortive gallop after Ryzhov's cavalry, resulting from no order at all but initiated by the shared aggression and energy of the ordinary horsemen who made up the five regiments. This incident would have been officially swept under the carpet to prevent adverse consequences for the men and to conceal Cardigan's own embarrassing lack of control over his men.

Either way, it is against this background that Cardigan's actions must be judged in order to weigh their true significance. As Raglan sent a series of orders to the bewhiskered Cardigan, he could scarcely have been unaware that his men were spoiling and clamoring for a fight; after all, if Doyle's testimony is correct, they had already charged en masse without orders merely at the sight of nearby battle and a tempting enemy target. Cardigan's problem was no so much how to get his men to attack against overwhelming odds but how to hold them back from doing so. When Raglan's fourth order arrived, he seemingly judged that it was impossible to do so any longer and gave official sanction to the action they likely would have taken without his approval anyway.

Raglan issued a large number of orders, most of which were simply disregarded by Lucan,

Cardigan, and others. Due to the sharp limits of communications and scouting in the days before radios and aerial reconnaissance, commanders on the spot were almost always given the option of refusing orders from distant superiors, whose information might be wrong or outdated. An army without radio simply could not remove all initiative from the front-line officers who were dealing with the actual situation in real time, and this included a general custom of allowing them to disobey orders without consequences as long as the situation merited this step.

Finally, Raglan sent an order to Lucan via his messenger Cpt. Nolan. This order, which arrived shortly before 11:00 a.m., read, "Lord Raglan wishes the cavalry to advance rapidly to the front – follow the enemy and try to prevent the enemy carrying away the guns – Troop Horse Artillery may accompany – French cavalry is on your left. Immediate." This order was appallingly vague because it gave no concrete objective, did not state which enemy was to be targeted, and did not even specify which guns the foe was to be prevented from carrying away. Considering the number of Russian units scattered across several miles of terrain, not to mention the gun batteries located at many points around the landscape, such an order could have been interpreted as meaning an attack on a wide range of equally plausible objectives.

Nevertheless, Lucan ordered the Light Brigade to advance and ordered Scarlett and the Heavy Brigade to support it. This is usually assumed to be the moment when blind obedience to orders took over, but when Lucan was censured over the affair, he made no effort to blame Raglan's orders while defending himself, which would have been a natural step to take if there were any truth to the idea. "Instead, he said in a letter to Lord Raglan that he obeyed it because not to do so would have 'exposed me and the cavalry to aspersions.'" (Small, 2007, Chapter 5).

On March 20th, 1855, *The Times of London* published a transcript of a hearing before the House of Lords during which various letters about Lucan's decision to attack were read to the House and important people offered their opinions. Commander in Chief, the Viscount Hardinge, in referring to Lucan's statements regarding his reasons for ordering the Charge of the Light Brigade, summarized his opinion of the lengthy debate in this way: "Surely, when the noble earl talks of possible aspersions, it shows that his decision to attack was taken, not upon any impression which he had of Lord Raglan's order, but upon the fear which he entertained of aspersions from his officers and soldiers." (Intelligence,1855, 5).

This constitutes strong (if not decisive) proof that Lucan and Cardigan obeyed Raglan's order to attack not because of absolute obedience to their superior's decrees (especially given the fact that they had openly ignored a number of other direct orders from him immediately beforehand) but because the order corresponded to what their men wanted to do and likely would do in the near future with or without permission. The Light Brigade was already seething with anger and was impatiently ready to hurl themselves headlong on the Russian cavalry visible at the far end of the North Valley, and Raglan's order simply gave Lucan and Cardigan a way to save face under color of an official order while actually acquiescing to the pressure of their fierce, ungovernable subordinates. Cardigan underlines this compulsion still further when he notes that "I received the order to attack from my superior officer in front of my troops." Cardigan is here asserting that his ordinary cavalrymen heard the order to attack given and thus implies that their knowledge of this prevented him from taking any action other than commanding his brigade to begin the charge.

The explanatory power of this notion is even further strengthened by the direction the charge took. Rather than attacking the nearest Russian batteries, the Light Brigade charged east along the North Valley towards Ryzhov's Russian cavalry, which now sat motionless at its eastern end behind a screen of guns, joined by the hated Cossacks. They had wanted to attack both of these bodies of Russian cavalry at different times during the day, and now they had the chance to bloody their sabers in combat with both simultaneously.

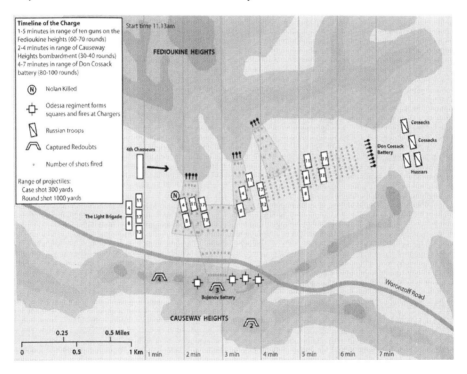

A map of the direction in which the charge was made

Far from the organized nature depicted in Tennyson's poem, the launch of the charge was not a smooth, uneventful process. Lucan was puzzled by the bizarre vagueness of Raglan's orders and asked Nolan which enemy he was to attack. Nolan responded with a contemptuous snarl of "there, my Lord, is your enemy; there are your guns," (Sweetman, 1995, 68), while gesturing vehemently up the North Valley, which infuriated Lucan. Nolan's dangerous insubordination silenced the lord, however, who had no wish to lose his dignity by conversing with him further. With that, the order to advance was given.

A depiction of Nolan

The first man into the North Valley was Cardigan himself, who showed a cool disregard for danger as he led his brigade forward. He carried his saber drawn and sloped back to rest on his right shoulder. The Light Brigade was deployed in three lines for the advance behind him. The first line consisted of the 13th Light Dragoons and the 17th Lancers on the right and left respectively. The 11th Hussars made up the second line, and the rear was brought up by the 8th Hussars on the right and the 4th Light Dragoons on the left.

A short distance behind this third line, Lucan and several members of his staff rode separately. Scarlett led the Heavy Brigade a few yards behind them, deployed, like the Light Brigade, in three successive lines. The first line was made up of the 1st Dragoons ("The Royals") on the right, and the magnificently accoutered 2nd Dragoons ("Scots Greys) on the left. The 6th

Dragoons, the Inniskillings, made up the second line. The 4th and 5th Dragoon Guards brought up the rear.

A picture of the terrain across which the charge was made (from left to right)

Very shortly after the charge began, with the men moving forward at an easy trot to spare their horses, the Russian artillery opened fire on this unexpected target. Batteries had been set up on the Fedioukine Heights on the valley's north flank and were present on the Causeway Heights along its south flank. More guns stood at the valley's head. The air began to be filled with the thunderous, deafening crashes of cannon discharges, the whining sound of shells and grapeshot cutting the air, and the bang of explosions. This tumult was soon joined by the popping sound of musket and the screams of wounded men and animals. Clouds of whitish-gray powder smoke billowed and drifted above the green, sunlit turf.

The fine weather which had assisted the Highlanders in finding easy marks among Ryzhov's cavalry in the South Valley earlier now helped the Russians adjust the aim of their guns. As flesh tore, blood spilled, and earth and grass was thrown skyward, the Light Brigade began to pick up speed without any order being necessary, even as shell fragments hissed through the air. All the men, Cardigan included, wanted to get through the curtains of steel and death and sink their sabers, lances, and carbine bullets into the hated Russian cavalry at the head of the North Valley.

It was at this point that Tennyson's poem captures the sheer violence and frantic energy of the attack, as well as the Russians' blistering enfilade:

"Cannon to right of them,

Cannon to left of them,

Cannon in front of them

Volleyed and thundered;

Stormed at with shot and shell,

Boldly they rode and well,

Into the jaws of Death,

Into the mouth of hell

Rode the six hundred."

Behind them, Lucan succumbed to overwhelming caution once again. Rather than charging the flanking batteries, or continuing to support the Light Brigade, "Lord Look-On" decided that there was no point in further advance. As soon as the first few men of the Heavy Brigade were blown into chunks of bleeding flesh by an exploding Russian shell, Lucan ordered the Heavy Brigade to first halt and then withdraw slightly. Though still holding a relatively advanced position, the Heavies were now to serve as a screen for the Light Brigade's retreat, and no more. General Scarlett, having caught a spark of the Light Brigade's mood, led the 5th Dragoon Guards forward without orders a little way down the North Valley, but they turned around when the rest of the Heavy Brigade failed to follow.

Further behind Scarlett, under the Sapoune heights, the Duke of Cambridge and Sir George Cathcart were deploying their infantry with all the slowness of a sloth. Neither would advance to support the Light Brigade, and they would actually wait for another 4-5 hours before even making a feeble demonstration in the direction of the Causeway Heights (which they were supposed to retake).

The Light Brigade's acceleration is also quite likely to have been due to sheer exuberance and aggression among many of its members. Several accounts provide confirmation of this eager, savage, hawkish mood. "The horses were as anxious to go as we were; mine snorted and vibrated with excitement," a participant named Grigg wrote (Small, 2007, Chapter 5). Other survivors spoke of a like spirit, such as one officer named Portal: "On we went at a steady pace at first, and then we saw the Russian cavalry retiring, so all the men cheered and went on at a gallop." (ibid).

At one point during the Charge, the 17th Lancers began to pull ahead of the 13th Light Dragoons. An NCO of the Dragoons roared, "Come on; don't let those bastards get ahead of us!" Thus, the 13th surged ahead in an effort to be the first to stick their blades in the enemy. This is not the reaction of stoic men resigned to death because of orders they do not actually wish to carry out but of military men urging one another on in a fierce rush towards human quarry.

During the early stages of the charge, Captain Nolan suddenly rode wildly out in front of the Light Brigade and gestured conspicuously. Though it is often speculated that he was attempting to redirect the charge towards the Causeway Heights (and this does seem likely), he did not survive long enough to deliver whatever message he wished to convey. His body was punctured by multiple iron shards from an exploding Russian shell, and his horse wheeled back through the lines. Drenched in his own blood, Nolan remained in the saddle for several seconds before toppling off into the grass with what one observer described rather strangely as "the shriek of a corpse." It is highly unlikely that the Light Brigade would have heeded Nolan in any case. The men and officers had already chosen their target in the form of Ryzhov's cavalry "skulking" behind the guns at the valley's eastern end, and Cardigan was merely along for form's sake.

The majority of those killed and wounded were struck during the initial ride up the Valley. Many men were also unhorsed and immediately turned around to make their way back to the British lines, which was sensible since they would be inevitably taken prisoner or executed by the Cossacks once their own side retired and they were still on foot in no man's land. Many accounts stress the violence of the fire directed at the British during their advance, such as the rather eccentric description offered by Sergeant John G. Baker, No. 888, of the 4th Light Dragoons: "We galloped through all this firing, which was almost as thick as hail, and the shot from the guns were almost as large as ordinary Dutch cheeses; and shells were bursting all around us." (Dawson, 2014, Chapter 5).

Nevertheless, despite many men and even more horses being struck, the Light Brigade held together during the whole seven minute advance and charged in among the guns at the end of the valley after receiving a final blast of canister shot at point blank range. They were finally within reach of the Russian gunners and the cavalry halted behind them, and they were ready to exact a deadly revenge for the day's frustrations and humiliations.

John Charlton's painting *Into the Valley of Death* (depicting the 17th Lancers reaching the Russian guns)

To the Russians manning the guns and the Cossacks immediately to their rear, the lines of British cavalry bursting out of the last choking veil of cannon-smoke were a nightmarish spectacle, appearing like an unstoppable juggernaut that had apparently just survived the impossible. The British hurled themselves on their opponents with animalistic fury, but with skill and coordination as well. As an unknown officer of the 17th Lancers wrote, "The Russian prisoners [...] say the Russians were petrified at the audacity of the attack and the energy that could after such a fire break through their lines" (Dawson, 2014, Chapter 5).

Tennyson described the scene at this point in his poem:

"Flashed all their sabres bare,

Flashed as they turned in air

Sabring the gunners there,

Charging an army, while

All the world wondered.

Plunged in the battery-smoke

Right through the line they broke;

Cossack and Russian

Reeled from the sabre stroke

Shattered and sundered."

In this regard, Tennyson's poem is highly accurate regarding the furious few minutes spent at the head of the North Valley. The British slaughtered the Russian gunners who attempted to resist and then plunged headlong into the Cossacks behind them. Ryzhov was about to prove himself the equal in incompetence of any British general; he had deployed a type of cavalry almost exclusively useful as skirmishers in an effort to stem the onrush of regular line cavalry. The Cossacks were adapted to loose hit-and-run action and were close to useless in a large-scale melee. Furthermore, Ryzhov met a charging enemy with motionless horsemen for the second time in a day, demonstrating clearly that he was not fit to command and had no understanding whatsoever of the nature of cavalry. A charge must be met with a charge or momentum will almost automatically give victory to the men in motion over those who are immobile.

The Cossack and Hussar units behind the guns did indeed "reel from the saber stroke, shattered and sundered." The Light Brigade smashed their immobile formation apart, cutting down men and animals and shooting some at point blank with their carbines, and the forward line of Russian cavalry turned and fled in a chaotic, panicking swarm towards the Chyornaya River in their rear.

However, there was another line of cavalry behind them, and at this point, the Light Brigade was finally forced to turn around or be overwhelmed by sheer numbers. One of the British officers from the 17th Lancers summed up the predicament succinctly: "It was a bitter moment after we broke through the line of cavalry in the rear of their guns, when I looked round and saw there was no support beyond our own brigade, which, leading in the smoke, had diverged, and scarcely filled the ground. We went on, however, and hoped that their own men flying would break the enemy's line ... When I saw them form four deep instead, I knew it was 'all up,' and called out to the men to Rally." (Dawson, 2014, Chapter 5).

As the officer points out, it was only at this moment that the Light Brigade realized they had no support. Lucan, succumbing to the dread of initiative which paralyzed the Allied high command throughout the war, had stopped the Heavy Brigade long before, and Sir George Cathcart was standing idle with his infantry just under the Sapoune Heights, ignoring all orders to advance. The Light Brigade had won a tactical victory in just seven minutes, punching through the Russian lines and giving a chance for the whole Czarist army to be defeated in detail if the gap was exploited. However, it was not exploited, and the Light Brigade, sensing that they had been abandoned by their own commanders, had no choice but to retreat despite their temporary success.

Chapter 7: The Retreat of the Light Brigade

Richard Caton Woodville's *The Relief of the Light Brigade* (depicting the 11th Hussars reaching the Russian guns)

Cardigan was one of the first of the Light Brigade to leave the field. The Earl had proven his courage amply, riding calmly through blasts of cannonballs and grapeshot, receiving a wound while attacking the Russian gunners, and then moving forward a bit further towards the Cossacks. One of the Russian commanders, Prince Radziwill, ordered the Cossacks to take him alive. No doubt fearing a slow death by the knout if they accidentally killed the British nobleman while capturing him, the Cossacks barely made an attempt to seize Cardigan, to the point that the Earl actually ignored them. Resting his sword on his shoulder again "at the slope," he simply rode out of the battle and down the valley, alone save for dismounted British cavalrymen fleeing on foot.

The rest of the Light Brigade soon followed, and it was at this point that the relatively small unit of 8 squadrons of French Chasseurs D'Afrique proved their merit. Seeing the plight of the

British, they offered the only outside support the Light Brigade received that day. The French horsemen formed up and charged the Russian batteries on the Fedioukine Heights on the north edge of the valley. They took the guns, killing the gunners in the process, but were unable to defeat the infantry squares beyond. Nevertheless, they greatly reduced the amount of artillery fire directed at the retreating Light Brigade.

A painting depicting the Chasseurs d'Afrique clearing Fedioukine Heights

A fresh body of between 1,000 and 2,000 Russian cavalry rode down from the Fedioukine Heights to attempt to block the retreat of the Light Brigade, but once again, the much smaller numbers of British smashed their way through the blocking force, which was made up of Uhlans, or lancers. Trumpeter Robert Nichol of the 8th Hussars provided a terse summation of this action in a letter to his father, writing, "We came Left About Wheel, and charged them, and very soon mowed our way through them." (Dawson, 2014, Chapter 5).

At this point, the Cossacks scoured the field, killing many of the wounded men that they found and taking a few prisoner. Out of the 675 men who started the charge, 118 were killed, 127 were wounded, and 60 were taken prisoner. 335 horses were killed or wounded so badly that they needed to be shot, but the loss of horses was only a temporary setback, despite the statements of some modern historians. As Private Samuel Walker of the 8th Hussars explained to his brother,

"Our regiment [is] now mounted on Russian horses, which we took from the Russian cavalry. They are a very good breed of horse […] we have taken some hundreds of them" (Dawson, 2014, Chapter 5).

Of course, a hurricane of recriminations followed the charge, predictably centered on who had ordered the attack (instead of the far more germane question of who had failed to support its successes properly). The men of the Light Brigade, at least, knew that they had executed their attack with verve and tactical success. When the regrouped survivors located Cardigan, he declared, "Men! It is a mad-brained trick, but it is no fault of mine." Once again, like the other senior British officers, Cardigan perceived taking initiative and attacking as problems, not keys to victory. "Never mind, my lord," an anonymous man called back from amid the gathered cavalry in their blood-stained, powder-darkened uniforms. "We are ready to go again."

Cardigan would later describe the charge to the House of Commons back in England:

> "We advanced down a gradual descent of more than three-quarters of a mile, with the batteries vomiting forth upon us shells and shot, round and grape, with one battery on our right flank and another on the left, and all the intermediate ground covered with the Russian riflemen; so that when we came to within a distance of fifty yards from the mouths of the artillery which had been hurling destruction upon us, we were, in fact, surrounded and encircled by a blaze of fire, in addition to the fire of the riflemen upon our flanks.
>
> As we ascended the hill, the oblique fire of the artillery poured upon our rear, so that we had thus a strong fire upon our front, our flank, and our rear. We entered the battery—we went through the battery—the two leading regiments cutting down a great number of the Russian gunners in their onset. In the two regiments which I had the honour to lead, every officer, with one exception, was either killed or wounded, or had his horse shot under him or injured. Those regiments proceeded, followed by the second line, consisting of two more regiments of cavalry, which continued to perform the duty of cutting down the Russian gunners.
>
> Then came the third line, formed of another regiment, which endeavoured to complete the duty assigned to our brigade. I believe that this was achieved with great success, and the result was that this body, composed of only about 670 men, succeeded in passing through the mass of Russian cavalry of—as we have since learned—5,240 strong; and having broken through that mass, they went, according to our technical military expression, "threes about," and retired in the same manner, doing as much execution in their course as they possibly could upon the enemy's cavalry. Upon our returning up the hill which we had descended in the attack, we had to run the same gauntlet and to incur the same risk from the flank fire of the Tirailleur as we had encountered before. Numbers of our men were shot down—

men and horses were killed, and many of the soldiers who had lost their horses were also shot down while endeavouring to escape.

But what, my Lord, was the feeling and what the bearing of those brave men who returned to the position. Of each of these regiments there returned but a small detachment, two-thirds of the men engaged having been destroyed? I think that every man who was engaged in that disastrous affair at Balaklava, and who was fortunate enough to come out of it alive, must feel that it was only by a merciful decree of Almighty Providence that he escaped from the greatest apparent certainty."

Chapter 8: Reasons for the Light Brigade's Combat Success

In the action which occurred at the head of the valley, at what might be termed the "high tide mark" of the Charge of the Light Brigade, the superiority of the British cavalry to that of the Russians is underscored in account after account. As already noted, the Charge could be counted as an initial success despite heavy losses, and it was only the failure of support to materialize (other than the attack of the French Chasseurs D'Afrique on the flanking batteries on Fedioukine Heights) that forced the Light Brigade to retreat under increasingly heavy counterattacks.

Several reasons are likely to account for the fact that approximately 670 British light cavalry, consisting of lancers and hussars, were able to rout roughly 2,000 Cossacks and supporting cavalry drawn up behind the artillery at the valley's head, then break through a further 1,000 or more Russian Uhlans who sought to impede or prevent their retreat a few minutes later. One highly important factor, of course, was the excellent training, fighting spirit, and discipline making up the intangible but critical phenomenon of "troop quality." The Russians were astounded and dismayed at the inexorable courage shown by the Englishmen, which unnerved them and gave the Light Brigade a morale advantage despite the brutal pounding its ranks underwent in "the Valley of Death." This advantage was summed up tersely in a letter from Sgt. William Garland of the 17th Lancers, who wrote that the British "only escaped (those who did) by reason of the cowardice of the Russians." (Dawson, 2014, Chapter 5).

The English were also trained to work well together, a military concept sometimes called "articulation." They closed their ranks immediately and rapidly when a man or horse fell without the need for orders, thus automatically presenting a united front bristling with swords and sabers (unlike the relatively chaotic Cossacks or poorly trained Russian line cavalry). Men trained in this fashion also act to protect the soldiers flanking them and assist with killing their opponents, turning the unit into a highly coordinated collective that can defeat much larger mobs of men who are fighting individually and offering each other little or no support. Teamwork is a powerful force in combat, particularly melee, and the British enjoyed a significant superiority to the Russians in this regard.

Another major factor in the British ability to shatter much larger formations of Russian cavalry appears to have been superior equipment and better mounts. There is something of a fad among some modern historians and novelists to praise the small, agile horses or ponies of the Mongol cavalry, the Cossacks, and similar horsemen. However, while it is true that these horses are better able to survive on sparse forage and reduced water rations, the men mounted on them were historically at a distinct disadvantage compared to those with larger and stronger cavalry mounts. This point is made clearly in a letter from a man known only as "G.C.", who wrote from the hospital in Scutari a week after the Battle of Balaclava that "their horses, little cats of things, could not stand the jumping forward of our powerful animals ... in short, both horse and horse-men are no match for ours." (Dawson, 2014, Chapter 5).

This was true only of the Cossack cavalry, since the Russian line cavalry (regular cavalry units) had much better horses, but much of the Light Brigade's force was directed at Cossack regiments, who found their formation broken apart and their mounts knocked down by the larger, stronger English animals. A larger, more powerful horse can also accelerate more rapidly and run more quickly over a short distance, even if the smaller horses hold a strategic advantage. This made it more difficult for the Cossacks to escape the British during the latter's attack, and it helped the Light Brigade overtake them when they were retreating.

Finally, the weaponry of the English also proved to be of higher quality and better design. The same G.C. provides a vivid description of the difference when he writes "such splendid cutting and thrusting never was seen; our heavy-Dragoon's swords are longer and straighter than the Russians', and about ten inches from the point they have a double edge; the Russian sword is a complete curve, and is not of the slightest use in giving point." (Dawson, 2014, Chapter 5).

It is axiomatic that point defeats edge in combat between swordsmen, a fact that has been recognized at least since the campaigns of Julius Caesar. A strike with the point is faster and harder to parry than a cut, and it is more likely to penetrate bulky clothing such as a hussar pelisse or a dragoon's tunic. A stab wound is also far more apt to be fatal or cause a disabling injury, penetrating internal organs and causing profuse bleeding, while a cut may penetrate no deeper than surface muscles. Thrusts are also far easier to execute in a dense crowd of fighting men, whereas a slash needs much more room to be delivered forcefully and dexterously.

In sum, multiple factors contributed to the remarkable superiority of the British cavalry to their Russian opponents. The British were better trained, had much higher morale, and exhibited a notable degree of teamwork and articulation, even without the need for orders. The Russians were unnerved by the valor of the English cavalry after their passage through the crossfire of multiple batteries, and the English horses were larger than Cossack steeds, allowing them to break up the Cossack formations and quite likely knock down the smaller horses in many instances. Finally, the straighter sword of the British gave them a crucial killing advantage in melee, reaffirming the immemorial primacy of point over edge.

Survivors from the 13th Light Dragoons after the charge

Picture of a 1904 reunion of survivors of the Light Brigade

Though Lord Tennyson's poem is a rousing piece that captures both the undoubted valor of the ordinary British cavalryman and the terrifying shock and furious energy of combat, it contains a fundamental distortion which has leaked over into serious histories of the conflict. Tennyson, exactly like the British high command, clearly considers the action as a blunder, and that inaction would have been a preferred solution to the situation. He "absolves" the British cavalry of the supposed "blunder" of attacking by shifting the "blame" for actually doing something onto their leaders.

In fact, it can be convincingly argued that the real blunder was not action but inaction. The significance of the Charge of the Light Brigade is that on one occasion, when the ordinary British soldiers and lower-ranking officers more or less bullied their commanders into launching an attack, that attack seared its way powerfully through much larger numbers of Russians. The entire army of Liprandi might have been broken and routed if support had been offered to the breakthrough, whether it was Sir George Cathcart advancing his infantry or the Heavy Brigade moving forward in support rather than halting and then withdrawing slightly.

The Charge also demonstrated that the British army was a deadly instrument that was permitted to flounder uselessly and die by inches due to the inability of its commanders to exploit an endless series of opportunities offered to them on a platter. Ironically, in a rather different way than the myth of the Charge of the Light Brigade would have people believe today, the cavalry action in the North Valley on October 25th, 1854 was just one in a long series of incidents which proved the accuracy of one Russian officer's possibly apocryphal judgment of the British as "lions commanded by asses."

Lord Tennyson's "The Charge of the Light Brigade"

"Half a league, half a league,

Half a league onward,

All in the valley of Death

Rode the six hundred.

'Forward, the Light Brigade!

'Charge for the guns!' he said:

Into the valley of Death

Rode the six hundred.

'Forward, the Light Brigade!'

Was there a man dismay'd?

Not tho' the soldier knew

Someone had blunder'd:

Theirs not to make reply,

Theirs not to reason why,

Theirs but to do and die:

Into the valley of Death

Rode the six hundred.

Cannon to right of them,

Cannon to left of them,

Cannon in front of them

Volley'd and thunder'd;

Storm'd at with shot and shell,

Boldly they rode and well,

Into the jaws of Death,

Into the mouth of Hell

Rode the six hundred.

Flash'd all their sabres bare,

Flash'd as they turn'd in air,

Sabring the gunners there,

Charging an army, while

All the world wonder'd:

Plunged in the battery-smoke

Right thro' the line they broke;

Cossack and Russian

Reel'd from the sabre stroke

Shatter'd and sunder'd.

Then they rode back, but not

Not the six hundred.

Cannon to right of them,

Cannon to left of them,

Cannon behind them

Volley'd and thunder'd;

Storm'd at with shot and shell,

While horse and hero fell,

They that had fought so well

Came thro' the jaws of Death

Back from the mouth of Hell,

All that was left of them,

Left of six hundred.

When can their glory fade?

O the wild charge they made!

All the world wondered.

Honour the charge they made,

Honour the Light Brigade,

Noble six hundred."

Bibliography

Chappell, Mike. *British Cavalry Equipments 1800-1941, Revised Edition.* Oxford, 2002.

Dawson, Anthony. *Letters from the Light Brigade: The British Cavalry in the Crimean War.* Barnsley, 2014.

Fraser, George MacDonald. *Flashman at the Charge.* London, 1986.

Intelligence, Parliamentary (newspaper column). "House of Lords, Monday, March 19." *The*

Times of London, March 20, 1855.

Kelly, Christine (ed.). *Mrs. Duberly's War: Journal & Letters from the Crimea.* Oxford, 2007.

Loy Smith, George. *A Victorian RSM.* Tunbridge Wells, 1987.

McGuigan, Ron. *Into Battle: British Orders of Battle for the Crimean War, 1854-56.* Bowden, 2001.

Small, Hugh. *The Crimean War: Queen Victoria's War with the Russian Tsars.* Slough, 2007.

Sweetman, John. *Balaclava 1854: The Charge of the Light Brigade.* London, 1995.

14731213R00028

Printed in Great Britain
by Amazon.co.uk, Ltd.,
Marston Gate.